Pull Up
A Chair

poems by
Kedan Harris

Pull Up A Chair
Copyright

ISBN   978-0-578-56118-9

Dedication

Some are long. Some are short,
But nothing close to a book report.
Just some thoughts with you to share.
Poems to be enjoyed, right here.

To my family,
and all who pulled up a chair
during writing.

Contents

Let's Reason

Pull up a chair. Let's reason.
Ponder over anything – in or out of season.
Let's move the needle, difficult or easy.
We can discuss 'til the day becomes breezy.

Let's engage, as if we had made a pact.
Trade thoughts. You then me. Forth and back.
Pull up a chair then. Let's see what's in store.
Oh, just one thing: please, don't scratch the floor.

Silence

Shut the door. Silence.
Close the window. Silence.
Turn the radio off. Silence.
Then what?
Sit there, listening to the gears in your head turn? Unnecessary.

Unlock the door. You invited them over.
Open the window. The birds are in symphony.
Tune the radio. Then get up and boogie-woogie.
But what's wrong with silence?
How else will I know if a gear has gone squeaky?

Absorbed in the Text

Don't let it just sit there. Open it.
Page after page a story unfolds within it.
Do battle with the ideas, the theme, the plot.
But you must first open it to explore the whole lot.

Thumb through. Smell the pages, how they are old or new.
Sense the emotions as if you were right there too.
Oh you can't put it down, for now you are absorbed in the text.
Look! You have read a book. Which one will you open next?

A Clever Thing

A poem takes a quicker route to the heart.
A cocktail of words – sheer art.
It can address the issues with the precision of a scalpel.
Introduce a drum, a horn. What can't it handle?

A poem is a clever thing.
Words arranged to pull you in.
Some are short and light – a ditty,
Others deep, telling, even pithy.

A poem is a loaded pill.
Swallow and let it thrill.
It is a waltz with figures of speech.
And from each read can new perspectives reach.

That Kind of Gift

Music is that kind of elixir
Where happiness lives in its mixture.
It can accomplish many things,
Whether through drum, guitar, or violin.
Music is that kind of gift.
It cures the spirit and it uplifts.
It brings vitality to the soul.
Each note, each riff, has a purposeful role.

Guitar Man

A man with a guitar had developed a repertoire,
Which was by far what made him a star.
No, not the kind of star who is popular,
But the one who stays true to the music.
For the people listening were rendered static
As he made the strings of that guitar wax poetic.

Who are You?

Who are you? Where are you from? Are you someone?
I am someone, from somewhere. I am!
I belong. My footprints were in the sand.
And once, I peed in the sea. No, twice.

You belong. You are from there. You are someone.
You planted that tree, still there at the foot of the dam.
You slipped in the mud when the rains came and blessed the
land.
And I saw you, once, by the shore. No, twice.

Pure Heart

What of hearts being dipped in love,
But one slipped and fell in?
Bathed completely, love stuck like a glove,
Leaving a rich, deep, stain within.
What can't a heart like that endure?
For it tends to give, share, and sacrifice.
Each beat, a pulse, vibrant and pure,
Oozing with innocence and free of vice.

Love

A whisper in the morning;
A nibble on the ear;
That gentle touch.

Fruits before breakfast;
Dinner on the deck;
Conversations about such and such.

A stroll in the evening;
Warm breeze on the cheeks;
Hands together, clutched.

Love, love, love.
Simple things
That mean so much.

Silhouette

Early, when that first light streaks into the room,
I glimpse you in silhouette on your side of the bed.
Stretched out, you sleep as if morning doesn't loom;
At peace, as that dream plays in your head.
Should I steal a kiss and risk your flinching,
Or wait 'til your movie ends and the credits are rolling?
But by then, that silhouette would have given way to colors
When light fills the room and you instinctively pull the covers.

Harmony

He wrote her poems – odes to her beauty;
Tributes to her warmth, her love, her unbending duty.
His words painted pictures she treasured in her heart.
Keeping them safe there, she did her part.

So when his words went away, leaving a dry well,
She opened her chest, releasing a flood, a veritable swell.
His eyes gleamed at each word she adoringly brought to voice;
Odes to his charm, his valor, his undeniable poise.

Formidable

Your body now aches.
It leans like a once-majestic palm.
How much more can it take?
Nerves just refuse to stay calm.
Yet, that mind of yours is as sharp!
And your quick wit, incomparable.
Though your eyes cover your world like a lousy tarp,
Still you endure with grace so formidable.

Where Tears Once Ruled

She's not of the opinion that a soft soul is efficient.
It serves no purpose that those tears with others be shared.
To her, storing them in a reservoir of pain is sufficient.
But if the poison should one day gush and her dam drains bare,
What would fill the void where those tears once ruled?
So she would rather seal her emotions deep in a cavern
Instead of reclaiming the bright eyes where her agony now pools.
Yet, give her time for those tears to recede and her passion discern.

Go On

When the wind blows, she shivers.
The gusts swoop down into the valley, tickling the river.
She sits by there on a rock, baiting the sun.
Nothing but blue sky; big sky, and it goes on and on and on.
On and on like the river, like the wind, like yesterday's rain.
The gusts thrust harder than before and she shivers again.
But she too will go on; her eyes on the river, her back against the wind.
On and on 'til the big sky ends and the tall trees begin.

Gone

They arrive, exploding into streaks across the glass, violently.
Where do they go when they slip beyond the edge of their
stage?
Veins of liquid – silky – deploying as if in a frenzied rage.
What is their mission before they exit so hastily?
None?

New waves arrive, ferociously, as the previous ones.
They land like asteroids, bursting onto the scene.
Fanning out, they go this way and that way with electric zeal.
Then, like the rain from which they came, they vanish. Gone?
Gone.

This Day

Squinting, I can barely see the blue expanse,
Much less the thin line between sea and sky.
Yet, feet sinking into the sunbaked powder, I advance.
Wind-whipped sand begins to fly,
And it stings – hard – like hundreds of nano-sized daggers.
But all the time I can't wait to dive into the warm water.
Now sun-drunk and shriveled, out of the sea I stagger.
I see footprints in the sand, under trees, all over.
They form a map of countless trails to and from the shore.
Sheltered under a tree, it is time for a meal: fish and festival.
Reggae fills the air and the surf no longer roars.
It's then I wish this day could be like a recurring decimal.

Sweet Gold

It runs down the arm to the elbow
Where it pools into a bulb of yellow.
Then it drips.
Hold that mango with a firm grip,
For juice like that – true nectar – is so sweet.
Now that the seed stands bare, the job is complete.
Take another; tear the skin; smell the perfume.
This golden goodness has to be consumed.

Quadrille

Hol' daag! And take your places.
The women have arrived in their traditional dresses.
The men have pulled off looking dapper.
Fresh, like the eyes of a just-caught snapper.

They come to dance quadrille, with fancy footwork and twirls.
Men, one hand behind their back; women's dress tails unfurl.
Spin, hip-swing, approach, and retreat.
See the couples move to the Mento beat.

Quadrille is an old-time dance slaves would perform.
They were trying to be jolly when the opposite was the norm.
The banjo stops now and the village gets quiet.
The couples will dance again at next year's fete.

In the Country

Life is different in the country.
There the past juts up against future history.
A glimpse into the way things were done:
Work by day then to the river for fun.
Old men sip milk-chased rum at Lena's shop.
And women in the market sell the yield from the crop.

Even the air is different in the country:
Fresh, like someone left a fridge open slightly.
The crisp newness of each morning, thanks to dew drops.
Sweetness from blossoms lingers after the breeze stops,
While aroma wafting from food on a wood fire
Is like a silent invitation to come, join in, savor.

Oh if I had lived in the country –
Outside from dawn 'til sun slips behind trees;
Roving 'round eating oranges from the orchard;
Running through a field and watching cows wouldn't be hard.
But with images still vivid of those country summers,
I know there is more to life there than these wide-eyed
memories.

Morning, In the Garden

Barefoot, I am on the front lawn sitting, knees up against chest.
The grass is green, thick, and full from the walkway to the fence.
The blades feel like just that – a spiky, spiny carpet – and they prick me,
But not in a bad way, not seriously, and only when I move slowly.
I have permission to be outside and I am in my drudging clothes,
Except for my sandals, which got wet when I turned on the garden hose.

A spider has spun a web, staking out a corner of the garden.
It is above where the soil stays damp until the sun shines there, then it hardens.
At the edge of the lawn by the flower bed, a frog sits, waiting.
With shifty eyes perched atop its bulgy head, it watches, surveying.
Two butterflies play mid-air, silent as the morning has been,
And I run around the hibiscus trees to see if my shadow keeps up or wins.

Of course it doesn't, but just keeps pace, and then I stop and tumble to the grass,
Only to now be face-to-face with that spider, and breathing fast.
The frog is startled and shlop, shlop, hops away, but the spider? No fear.
It delicately rides the waves now rippling across its silken lair.
I retreat, deciding it's better where I was on the lawn, sitting, knees up against chest,
At least until all the garden creatures are back at rest.

Just Being Their Best

We always had dogs at our house.
Butch and Braniff loved to play and were easy to rouse.
Toby had short legs, so I dubbed him my Corgi.
Kibbles and Bits were the duo with names out of the ordinary.

Juno was a gift from uncle, before he left for England.
To us children she seemed tall as a horse, this Alsatian.
She loved the beach and taking a bath,
And could scale the fence with a running start.

We had a dog that was pleasant, though quite resolute.
One day she bit at Dad's foot, save for his leather boot.
He said: "Don't worry, she's just protecting her litter.
That's what they do until their young ones get bigger."

I loved our dogs and we would romp for hours,
Chasing 'round the yard and through Mum's flowers.
Our dogs slept in a kennel in the corner of the yard,
And after a day of fun, leaving them there was hard.

But it was funny when they ventured into the house,
Crossing that threshold then trying to sneak like a mouse.
Click, click, click, click: nails against tiles were a dead giveaway.
"Ok, you've caught me," the look in their eyes seemed to say.

A pat on the head and a rub of the belly was all they needed.
But when they barked, it was a warning to be heeded.
Our house, on the corner, probably needed no address.
It was the one with the dogs, just being their best.

Change of Mind

Never really cared for cats –
Selfish, self-centered, narcissistic, brats.
Try petting them and they dodge your hand,
As if to say: "No, no, no. You don't get to touch me, man."

But along came this one cat, a black and white with polydactyly.
He walked into our lives and changed my mind completely.
Rubbing his head on everything, the way cats do,
Making it clear: "Friends? Yes, I want to."

He became part of the family, even had a spot on the couch.
We treated him like a son, and for his loyalty we could vouch.
What fine company he became, enjoying all sorts of games.
Unselfish and loving: these qualities made his name.

Little Bird

The day the little bird died,
All of us children cried
At Mona Chapel Basic School.

Who knew that little thing
Would so much joy bring.
But then we found it, feet up and body cool.

Bye, bye little bird.
We'll press on, undeterred,
And be the exception to the rule.

Four Eyes

He stands there in the garden, curly hair and pug nose,
Trying hard to see, in his cartoon-covered clothes.
From that early age, there was trouble with his sight,
So people said: "He could never fly a plane, maybe only a kite."
But soon the little boy would be fitted with glasses,
And would sit in school at the front of all his classes.
"Four eyes! Four eyes!" "But aren't they better than two?"
He wore those glasses dutifully and learned, and grew, and grew.

Age Quod Agis

"You are Wolmerian now," he announced, over loud speaker:
Mr. Barnett, the school's fearless leader.
There in general assembly, heart racing, but so eager.
Maroon and gold epaulets emblazoned on both shoulders.
Khaki shirt and long pants: high school is big-boy stuff.
"Only the best," he said, "would be good enough."

Math and English in the morning;
Third-form History with Mrs. Spalding.
"Good Morning Señor Cesar," had to be our greeting
Before his Spanish lessons could get going.
Shakespeare, Chaucer, the Metaphysical poets.
Ms. Leyow rocked literature and we knew it.

"Fight! Fight!" Two guys go at it over some silly competition.
Lunchtime was more than cocoa bread, patty, or sugar bun.
PE, on the field, could be football, track, or cricket.
It depended on the sports season and we looked forward to it.
And though for a time, it was known as the Dust Bowl,
That field was central to our life at school.

"Wolmer's! Wolmer's!" We are at Champs again.
Our athletes run fast and their javelins are well-aimed.
But the day the fire tore through the place taking a lot of
history,
Wolmer's only rose like the Phoenix, stronger, in true victory.
So for all who attend this Heroes' Circle oasis,
The venerable motto to defend is: Age Quod Agis.

The Repeat

Get up. Prepare. Deep breath. Get out there.
Walk. To the left. Take a right. Train fare.
Smile. Sign in. Shake hands. Say hello.
Type. Submit. Swipe. Sign below.
Meet again. Read. Delete. Keep.
Get in. Unwind. Reflect. Fall asleep.

Bliss

Don't let me fall asleep in public,
Whether on a train, plane, or in the passenger seat.
For the times when I just can't fight it,
Sure enough, eyes roll back and mouth splits.
Some say it's not a pretty sight by any measure.
But tired, have you never yearned for that pleasure?
Then let me fall asleep, even in public.
Those precious moments of bliss are well worth it.

Odd Socks

I don't want to get up at six o'clock,
Just to get a leg-up in the hunt for that missing sock.
How can pairs linked together manage to come out the wash single?
During the spin cycle, do they dislodge and begin to mingle?

Now I have a drawer full of socks: black, blue, grey, and brown.
And the thought of having to sort them all, brings a smile? No, a frown.
I can't say my socks are like the famous two peas in a pod.
They always end up completely mixed up, which I just don't get. Odd.

Principled Shower

Water jets from the showerhead
In a manner quite unlike gentle dew.
A quick adjustment to the heat,
And it's sweet, through and through.
I wet my face, then go all under,
Thinking: "I could stay here for a while."
Sufficiently soaked and with eyes still closed,
I reach for a bar of Zest, Coast, or is it Dial?

Now this mini waterfall has swallowed me up,
And I'm ensconced within its liquid cocoon.
Here, you can get a lot of thinking done.
Look! I've planned my day, right up 'til noon.
But I end it soon, turn the water off
And step out onto the tile,
Just so as not to hear some cheeky voice declare:
"He runs the water, like it's his own River Nile."

Those Sounds

Cough. "Who did that?"
Sneeze. "Who is spreading that?"
Fart. "Who is owning that?"
Burp. "Who was that?"
"Just a regular human, making the sounds of life."

Morning, On a Bus

As it rounds a corner, you hold on tight, so as not to lose your
footing.
But it's way more than whether you are standing or by a
window sitting.
On a bus, you can observe people and guess what they might
be thinking.
The woman in the business suit, is it today that she's
interviewing?
She could be contemplating how best to impress, but now her
phone is ringing.
As she takes the call, a kid with a ball walks down the aisle
grinning.
You wonder: "What's so funny to make him so sunny this
early in the morning?"

Why drive a car, when riding a bus is by far more interesting?
No need to give attention to red, yellow or green, you are not
the one navigating.
On a bus, you can be productive, immersed in reading, writing,
or listening.
But then you can't ignore, with each opening of the door, the
people coming and going.
Who is that man coming with bag and pan? Is he with
homelessness contending?
He sits beside a fellow wearing a shirt quite yellow, who is
fast asleep and snoring.
You now begin to reflect and even start to reject some biases
you've been harboring.

Rounding another corner, you grab hold even tighter and
your mind continues churning.
It's now down to twenty people and still you are pondering:
"Where might they be heading?"

But more than that you realize they all have stories they could be telling.

By now Betty's palms are sweaty as she gets off at where she'll be interviewing.

Randy is always quite dandy, says him mom, who warns him about the ball he's bouncing.

And at the next stop is Peter's shelter. It's very helter-skelter, but he's coping.

Finally, the bus enters the terminus and you wonder: "Will I see them again?" "Not if you're driving."

Travels

I think of Kingston:
The hot spot; vibrant, trendy, bustling.
From people in cool high rises closing deals to fruit vendors on
the street hustling.

I think of Boston,
Where history and innovation coexist,
And where people love their sports: Red Sox, Patriots. Season
tickets.

I think of Praia
And the colonial shadow that was cast.
Look closely: each cobblestone bears footprints from the past.

I think of London
And the global impact of this one capital.
Palaces and museums and red buses and tea. Multicultural.

I think of Havana:
How it's more than a visible time capsule.
Compelling architecture to explore. Vintage cars galore. Mar
azul.

I think of Hamilton, Yarmouth, Freeport, Cancun:
Places people go to get away.
Yet, to travel is also to learn, even while on vacay.

Patois (Patwa)

Mi neva learn Patwa langwij inna school.
As a likkle bwoy, Standard English was di rule.
Patwa? Dem nevah really incurrij wi fi speak it –
Sumting 'bout bein' prapah an etikwet.
But mi nuh have nuh problem wid Patwa.
It nice fi tell story and fi gi joke inna.
Like when wan oohman name Merle guh ah Merka,
Shi ketch up wid har boss weh name Linda.
When Merle staat fi cuss an fling di Patwa,
Linda stan up amazed an shi jus ah stutta.
Merle staat fret now seh shi lose di likkle rurk,
Ungle fi hear Linda seh: "Can you repeat those Jamaican
proverbs?"
Mi laaf haad wen mi hear da won deh.
Patwa nice, man – even pon Sundeh.
But wait. Nuh figget bout English needa.
Eh, chroe likkle 'Panish side a dem two lingwa
An likkle fran dis, evri baddi a guh versatile.
Waah gwaan? What's happening? ¿Que pasa? Pop style!

We, The Same

Woke up, thinking I was in Jamaica:
Heard birds, dogs, and voices below the window.
It wasn't Kingston, but another capital, a place called Praia,
And the voices were making the sounds of Kriolu.
Bom dia. Sta fixi?: Good morning. All's well?
Visit Cabo Verde and you'll have much to tell.
Morabeza describes the people, for they are truly hospitable,
And like in Jamaica, everyone there just wants to feed you.
Katxupa on Saturday; this meal takes hours to prepare.
First caipirinha at Kebra Kanela, and Strela for beer.
In Patois, Jamaicans say: Nyam yuh food.
In Kriolu, nhemi means chew.
And while Jamaica is one island, Cabo Verde has nine, plus one.
But at the end of the day, it's all the same: "No problem, mon."

Ngosta

Ngosta di obi Kriolu.
Djan prendi tcheu.
Mas, a mi ka e di Fogo,
E nha nome ka e Joao.
Ngosta di tudo comida.
Kenki fazi ponche?
Nlembrá nha tenpu na Praia,
Mas, a mi nka odja kasobodi.
Sim, a mi e di Jamaica,
Pais di Bob Marley.
Si el baba a visita cada ilha
El flaba: One love, pamodi amizade.
Nton, nos tudo é Kriolu:
Ngosta nhos cultura,
De Campana di Baxo
A monti di Asomada.

It

Nah. That's bogus!
This thing must be allowed to grow like fungus?
Put it in a box and cut some tape,
But keep a close eye, lest it shifts shape.
Why not load it onto a boat bound for sea,
Or bury it in the forest at the foot of a tree?
Don't keep feeding it, so that it withers.
Whatever it is, hurry, before it slithers.

Enough Said

Brutality? No, never.
Humanity? Yes, forever.
You disagree? Whatever.

Undo

I see the blood upon the wall
From which the maggots fall.
Innocent blood, shed savagely.
Blood of victims who fell silently.
Forgotten? No, they are not.
The Creator will undo all this rot.

Keep Doing

What can you not do?
You know how to make it through.
Apply those skills and others will ensue.
Keep doing the things you know how,
And those goals you have, no time like now.
It's head up, forward, shoulder to the plow.

Lion Heart

Here is a man on a mission.
Moving with a lion's intuition.
Don't try to stop him or get in his way.
His mind is made up: today is his day.
So when you see him, watch for those eyes.
See how he is focused; sights on that prize.

Affinity

I will be there. It is as much as a guarantee.
If not in minutes, then at least in thought.
For who could share such affinity
And not appreciate the battle well-fought?